D.I.Y. MAKE IT HAPPEN

ART SHOW

VIRGINIA LOH-HAGAN

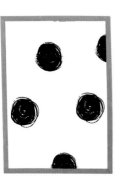

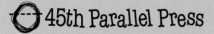

45th Parallel Press

Published in the United States of America by Cherry Lake Publishing
Ann Arbor, Michigan
www.cherrylakepublishing.com

Reading Adviser: Marla Conn, ReadAbility, Inc.
Book Designer: Felicia Macheske

Photos Credits: © Shots Studio/Shutterstock.com, cover, 1; © hebeko/Shutterstock.com, cover, 1; © Wolna-luna/Shutterstock.com, cover, 1; © Peter Svetoslavov/Shutterstock.com, 3; © Adriano Castelli/Shutterstock.com, 5; © Stephen Orsillo/Shutterstock.com, 7; © Grzegorz Petrykowski/Shutterstock.com, 9; © MR. INTERIOR/Shutterstock.com, 10; © Norman Pogson/Shutterstock.com, 11; © Gustavo Frazao/Shutterstock.com, 11; © White Room/Shutterstock.com, 12, 31; © Pressmaster/Shutterstock.com, 14; © donydony/Shutterstock.com, 15; © Leftleg/Shutterstock.com, 17; © LiliGraphie/Shutterstock.com, 18; © yurchello108/Shutterstock.com, 19; © Ilya Zonov/Shutterstock.com, 19; © GeniusKp/Shutterstock.com, 19; © BlueSkyImage/Shutterstock.com, 20; © Andrey_Kuzmin/Shutterstock.com, 21; © HandmadePictures/Shutterstock, 22; © TommL/iStock, 23; © Odua Images/Shutterstock.com, 27; © Shots Studio/Shutterstock.com, 28; © Tatiana Popova/Shutterstock.com, 29; © cosma/Shutterstock.com, 30; © wavebreakmedia/Shutterstock.com, back cover; © Dora Zett/Shutterstock.com, back cover

Graphic Elements: © bokasin/Shutterstock.com, cover, 1, 11, 19; © topform/Shutterstock.com, cover, back cover; 1; © pashabo/Shutterstock.com, 6, back cover; © axako/Shutterstock.com, 7; IreneArt/Shutterstock.com, 4, 8; © Belausava Volha/Shutterstock.com, 12, 20; © Nik Merkulov/Shutterstock.com, 13; © Ya Tshey/Shutterstock.com, 14, 27; © kubais/Shutterstock.com, 16; © Sasha Nazim/Shutterstock.com, 15, 24; © Ursa Major/Shutterstock.com, 23, 28; © Infomages/Shutterstock.com, 26; © Art'nLera/Shutterstock.com, back cover

45th Parallel Press is an imprint of Cherry Lake Publishing.

Library of Congress Cataloging-in-Publication Data

Loh-Hagan, Virginia.
  Art show / by Virginia Loh-Hagan.
    pages cm. — (D.I.Y. Make It Happen)
  Includes bibliographical references and index.
  ISBN 978-1-63470-494-6 (hardcover) — ISBN 978-1-63470-554-7 (pdf) — ISBN 978-1-63470-614-8 (pbk.) — ISBN 978-1-63470-674-2 (ebook)
  1. Art—Exhibitions—Juvenile literature. I. Title.
  N4395.L64 2016
  707.5—dc23
                              2015026838

Cherry Lake Publishing would like to acknowledge the work of The Partnership for 21st Century Skills.
Please visit www.p21.org for more information.

Printed in the United States of America
Corporate Graphics Inc.

ABOUT THE AUTHOR

Dr. Virginia Loh-Hagan is an author, university professor, former classroom teacher, and curriculum designer. She loves making art. She created an art nook in her house. She lives in San Diego with her very tall husband and very naughty dogs. To learn more about her, visit www.virginialoh.com.

TABLE OF CONTENTS

CHAPTER ONE

WHAT DOES IT MEAN TO HOST AN ART SHOW?

Do you love making art? Do your friends love to paint or draw? Do you love fancy parties? Then hosting an art show is the right project for you!

Art show hosts are also called **curators**. They choose art. They're in charge of an **exhibition**. An exhibition is a show. It introduces art to an **audience**. An audience refers to people who see a show.

Art show hosts share art with the world. They promote art. They show off art. Some make art as well.

An art **gallery** is a place that has art. An art show is an event. It focuses on a collection of art.

Attend other art shows to get ideas.

KNOW THE LINGO

Acid-free: paper that has no acids; acids can discolor art

Atelier: an artist's studio

Calligraphy: fancy lettering

Contemporary: art made by living artists

Cropping: editing a picture by removing outer edges

Genre: a category of artistic practice having similar techniques, form, or content

Happening: a performance, event, or situation considered as art

Limited edition: a set number of identical artworks numbered in order and signed by the artist

Mannered: having or showing a certain style

Monoprint: one-of-a-kind print by an artist

Open edition: a series of art that has an unlimited number of copies

Original: authentic work, not a copy

Plinth: the pedestal on which a sculpture is displayed

Provenance: record of ownership for a work of art

Remarque: additional enhancement by the artist on final prints

Salon: a gathering of artists, writers, and musicians in someone's home

Art shows are popular all year long. Curators and artists host art shows when they have new art. Artists hope to sell their art.

Many people host art shows to raise money for causes. They charge admission to the show. Or they try and sell the art. You can charge a small fee to come to the art show. Or you can ask for **donations**. This is when people give you money. They decide how much to give.

You'll have fun hosting your own art show. You'll make art. You'll show your friends' art. The best part is the opening night party. Your friends and family will celebrate art.

Assign someone to be in charge of handling money.

7

CHAPTER TWO

WHAT DO YOU NEED TO HOST AN ART SHOW?

First, decide if you want a group show or a **solo** show. A group show features several artists. More people would come to your show. A solo show features one artist. Think about the following:

→ Do I know enough artists to have a group show? Would my friends want to help create art for a show?

→ Do I only want to feature my work? Do I know enough people to come to my show?

→ Do I have enough art for my own show?

Second, choose a **theme**. A theme is a topic. The theme focuses the show.

➡ **Brainstorm a list of themes. You could focus on a style. You could focus on content.**

➡ **Choose your favorite idea.**

➡ **Think of an exciting name for your show.**

Focus your art show. Art shows usually have themes.

Decide where you want to host your art show.

➡ **Consider places available to you. Some examples are your house or school.**

➡ **Consider asking libraries, coffee shops, and restaurants.**

➡ **Make sure the space has walls.**

➡ **Make sure it has enough room. People need to walk around.**

➡ **Make sure it has space for your party.**

An adult can help you find a space for the show.

Decide on a time for your show.

➡ Decide how long you want to hang your art. Some shows last for several weeks.

➡ Decide when you want your opening night party. It's best over the weekend.

Create and send out invitations. Tell everybody!

➡ Make posters and **flyers**. Flyers are papers with event information.

➡ Use the Internet. Use e-mail.

YOU'RE INVITED!

Hosting an art show is like planning an event. Making lists helps you organize. Check off things as you complete them.

➡ Collect art. Make art yourself. Or get art from friends and artists. Protect the artwork. Get information about each piece.

➡ Collect things needed to hang art. You'll need frames. You'll need label cards. You'll need hammers and nails. You'll need rulers.

➡ Collect things needed for your party. You'll need decorations. You'll need drinks and snacks. You'll need napkins, cups, and plates.

Give yourself plenty of time to collect art.

TRY THIS!

Create an interactive art center for your opening night party. This will keep guests busy. Guests will be excited to make art.

You'll need: large white butcher paper, paints and paintbrushes, smocks, colored pencils, crayons, colored markers, art theme cards.

Steps

1 Choose a section of the room. Tape butcher paper to the wall.

2 Set up a station with art tools.

3 Create art theme cards. Guests pick a card and draw something related to that theme (examples: circles, spring, hope).

4 Allow guests to take turns drawing.

5 When there's no white space left, remove the artwork. Frame it. Sign it as "Opening Night Guests." Date it.

6 Add more paper. Start again!

You'll need help for your party. Get some friends. Assign them jobs. These are examples of some tasks:

Before people come:

➡ **Frame the art.**

➡ **Hang the art.**

➡ **Prepare drinks and snacks.**

When people come:

➡ **Greet them at the door. (Collect payment if you are charging.)**

➡ **Walk around with trays of snacks and drinks.**

➡ **Collect people's trash.**

After people leave:

➡ **Clean the area.**

Have your friends wear white shirts and black pants. This makes the party fancier!

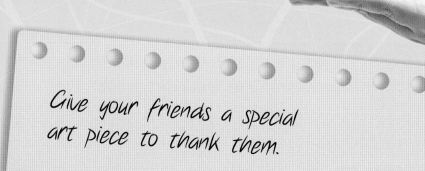

Give your friends a special art piece to thank them.

CHAPTER THREE

HOW DO YOU SET UP AN ART SHOW?

The point of an art show is to show art! So, have a good collection.

- Think about the art **medium**. Medium is the material used to create art. Will you include sculptures? Will you include paintings and drawings? Will you include photographs? There are many choices.

- Collect art that supports your theme.

- Choose the best pieces.

- Choose enough art to fill your space. A good show has at least 20 to 30 pieces.

- Choose art of different sizes.

- Create a **catalog**. A catalog is a book. It lists all the art. It lists information about each art piece.

LISA ABERNATHY

Lisa Abernathy is an artist. She does papercuts and textile work. Textiles are fabrics. She lives in Charleston, South Carolina. She has curated several art shows. She hosts "underground" art shows. These take place in restaurants, coffee shops, and alleyways. She's also shown her work at parking lots, barns, and churches. She advises to look for all kinds of **venues**. Venues are spaces. She said, "Non-traditional venues invite people to reinvent how they see art and the spaces in which it can be held. Galleries and museums are illuminating sites, but a coffee shop or [restaurant] can be more comfortable to someone who is new to the art world. The best part is our shows often stay up for a month and get exposure to anyone who wanders in."

Make sure artists sign their names on their art pieces.

Once you get the art, frame it. Framing makes art look professional. It makes it look finished.

➡ Consider using a **mat**. A mat is an extra border. It provides space around the art. It draws people's attention to the art.

➡ Choose a frame. Frames come in all shapes and sizes. Buy frames at stores. Buy frames at yard sales. Repaint frames for a fresh look.

➡ Include a wire on the back of framed art. This is for hanging.

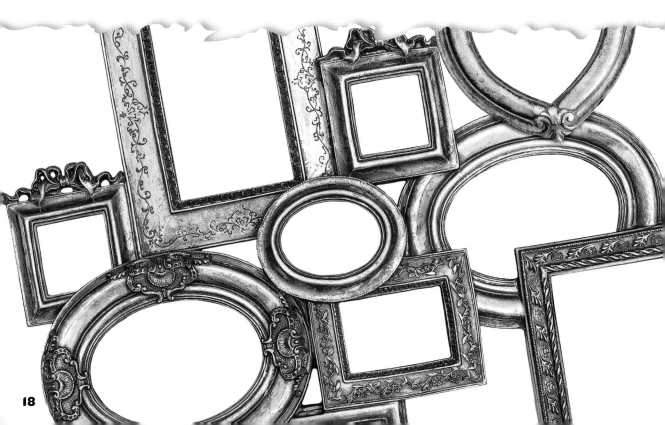

For each art piece, create a label card. Type it. Or ask someone with nice handwriting to help. Each label has the following information:

➡ **Title of artwork**

➡ **Name of artist**

➡ **Medium**

➡ **Price (if you're selling it)**

Provide stands for sculptures and other 3-D art.

Ask permission before hammering any nails into walls.

Hanging art is also called **installing**.
Make sure the art is nicely displayed.

➡ Decide how you want to group the pieces. You can group by artist. You can group by medium. You can group by topics.

➡ Decide how far apart you want the pieces. Spacing will depend on your place. You don't want pieces too close to each other. Give people room to view each art piece.

➡ Hang the pieces around eye level.

➡ Use lighting. Some art show hosts buy special lights. They hang lights above the art.

➡ Hang the label next to the art.

➡ Use a ruler to measure where you're hammering nails.

Host a special party. It celebrates the opening night of your art show. This is the first night people see your art.

➡ **Set up a table for greeting people. Put name tags and pens at that table. Put the catalog there.**

➡ **Make a playlist. The music should be calming.**

➡ **Provide drinks. Serve something with bubbles. Sparkling apple cider is an example. Use clear plastic cups.**

➡ **Provide snacks. Make finger sandwiches. Get cheese and crackers. Make cookies.**

➡ **Set up a snack table. Have friends act as servers. They walk around with food and drinks. They collect trash.**

➡ **Put trash cans around the room.**

Prepare a program of the night's events.
Include the following:

➡ **List of art and artists.**

➡ **List party events. Include speeches.**

Keep people looking at the art.

CHAPTER FOUR

HOW DO YOU RUN AN ART SHOW?

You've sent the invitations. You've set everything up. You're ready for the big night!

Pay attention to your **guests**. Guests are people who come to a hosted event.

→ Greet guests as they come in.

→ Ask them to fill out a name tag.

→ Tell them to help themselves to snacks and drinks.

→ Guide them to various art pieces.

→ Tell them about each art piece.

→ If you're hosting a group show, introduce guests.

- ➡ **Walk around. Talk to as many guests as possible. Don't stay in one place for too long. Interact with different people.**

Give guests plenty of time to look at art. Give people time to **mingle**. Mingle means hanging out. Art shows are social events. Consider giving a speech.

- ➡ **Give a quick speech about the theme. Talk about how and why you curated the pieces. Share interesting facts.**

- ➡ **For a group show, introduce the artists. Call them by name. Clap for each person.**

- ➡ **Thank your friends. Thank everyone who helped you. Clap for each person.**

- ➡ **Consider making a toast. Have everybody raise their glasses. Say nice things about art. Everyone drinks at the same time.**

- ➡ **Ask guests if they have questions about the art.**

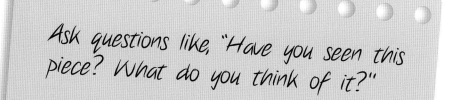

Ask questions like, "Have you seen this piece? What do you think of it?"

QUICK TIPS

- Get clothespins. (Decorate the clothespins!) Get string or wire. Create hanging art exhibits.

- You don't have to use picture frames. Other options are pants hangers, clipboards, and canvas with painted edges.

- Consider hosting a juried art show. A jury is a group of experts. Have them judge the art. Provide awards for different categories. Provide prizes.

- Create smaller prints or cards of your artwork. Use a copy machine. Sell them at your art show.

- After your art show ends, host an art auction. An auction is a public sale. Items go to the person who pays the most. Auctions are a good way to raise money for your school.

- Put a painted picture frame over corkboard. Pin artwork on it.

- Get some large boxes. Stack them on top of one another. Paint them. Put artwork on all four sides. You have an art tower!

- Get creative with themes. (Examples: tiny art, moving art)

Introduce people to each other.

If you are selling art, create a system for people to buy it. Don't be a salesperson. Let the art sell itself.

⇒ Mark the prices on the labels.

⇒ Assign a friend to handle payments.

⇒ Create a **receipt**. This is a proof of purchase.

⇒ Put a "Sold" sticker on the label of the artwork you sell. Don't let guests take the art. Wait until the show is over.

When guests leave, thank them for coming.

➡ **Ask guests to fill out feedback forms. Have them write what they liked about your art show.**

➡ **Get their contact information.**

➡ **Tell them to come back to your next art show!**

Send thank-you cards to people who bought your art.

D.I.Y. EXAMPLE!

STEPS	EXAMPLES
Type	Group art show
Theme	"Happy dogs"
Where	Local library
When	◆ Opening party on Saturday afternoon ◆ One-month art show
Fees	◆ Write prices on the labels. ◆ Include my contact information. (People can buy the art by contacting me. They can take the art home after the show is over.)
Make lists	◆ Make a list of things I need to get. ◆ Make a list of things I need to do.

STEPS	EXAMPLES
Collect art	• Collect art in all mediums. • Collect pieces that support the theme. • Feature at least six artists.
Frame art	• Spray-paint frames a gold color. String wire across the back of each. • Create an art tower (see Quick Tips)
Install art	• Frame artwork. Attach to walls. • Tape artwork to art tower. • Place sculptures on pedestals.
Host opening night party	• Ask a friend to play piano during the party. • Invite people to post a picture of their dogs on a bulletin board. Create a collage. • Make a toast to our dogs!

GLOSSARY

audience (AW-dee-uhns) people who see a show

catalog (KAT-uh-lawg) a book listing information

curators (KYOOR-ay-turz) people who collect and choose art

donations (doh-NAY-shuhnz) gifts of money

exhibition (ek-suh-BISH-uhn) show

flyers (FLYE-urz) advertisements; papers with event information

gallery (GAL-ur-ee) place that has art

guests (GESTS) people who come to a hosted event

installing (in-STAWL-eng) hanging

mat (MAT) extra border that provides space around an art image

medium (MEE-dee-uhm) material used to make art

mingle (MING-uhl) to hang out

receipt (ri-SEET) proof of purchase

solo (SOH-loh) alone

theme (THEEM) topic or idea

toast (TOHST) saying nice things in honor of something or someone and drinking together

venue (VEN-yu) a place where an event is held

INDEX

LEARN MORE

BOOKS

National Gallery of Art. *An Eye for Art: Focusing on Great Artists and Their Work*. Chicago: Chicago Review Press, 2013.

Schwake, Susan, and Rainer Schwake (photographer). *Art Lab for Kids: 52 Creative Adventures in Drawing, Painting, Printmaking, Paper, and Mixed Media*. Beverly, MA: Quarry Books, 2012.

WEB SITES

WikiHow—"How to Set Up an Art Exhibition": www.wikihow.com/Set-Up-an-Art-Exhibition